Are you ready for an Art Attack?

Step outside and get ready for some great garden-themed Art Attacks! Take a look at the natural world around you next time you're in the garden or taking a walk in the park. From flower power to autumn colours and fabulous frosty mornings, you'll be amazed at how much nature has to offer. Follow the steps to create a wonderful outdoor world in the comfort of your own home!

CONTENTS

Editor: Angela Hart
Designer: Joanna England
Artists: Mary Hall and Paul Gamble
Model Maker: Angela Hart

TREE STUMP HOUSE!

MAKE A TINY WOODLAND HOME FOR YOUR TOYS!

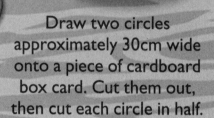

1 Draw two circles approximately 30cm wide onto a piece of cardboard box card. Cut them out, then cut each circle in half.

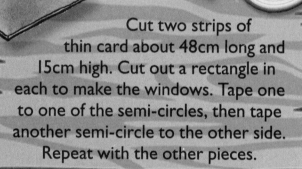

2 Cut two strips of thin card about 48cm long and 15cm high. Cut out a rectangle in each to make the windows. Tape one to one of the semi-circles, then tape another semi-circle to the other side. Repeat with the other pieces.

3 Tape the two pieces together to make a hinge, as shown.

4 Cover the whole thing in two layers of papier maché, building up the outside edges to look like stones or roots. Leave it to dry.

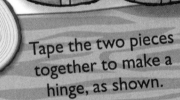

5 Paint the top of the tree stump with pale brown rings. The sides of the tree stump should look like bark, so use dark shades of brown and black. Paint the inside in natural colours and add a rug and a door.

4

6 Glue two plastic or acetate squares over the windows, then paint window frames. Cut out two small pictures from an old magazine and frame them with painted paper strips, then stick them to the walls.

7 To make the furniture, cut simple pieces of card and tape them together. Cover in two layers of papier maché and leave them to dry. Paint them however you like.

IN THE CAN!

1 Cut two circles of thick card about 20cm in diameter. Cut a semi-circle out of one of the circles, about 4cm in from the edge. Cut a piece of thin card 62cm long and 30cm high and tape it around the full circle of card. Tape the other piece to the top.

2 Cut two strips of thin card about 5cm wide and tape these on as shown to make the handles.

3 Cut an angle at one end of a kitchen roll tube and tape it to the body of the watering can to form the spout.

4 Draw around a small foil dish onto thin card, cut out the circle and tape it to the foil dish to make the shower head. Tape this to the kitchen roll tube.

5

Cover the whole thing in two or three layers of papier mâché and leave it to dry.

YOU WILL NEED:

Thin card, thick card, safety scissors, PVA glue, masking tape, kitchen roll tube, medium foil pie dish, paints, paintbrush.

6

Paint your watering can whatever colour you like and add some flowers for decoration.

YOU CAN DECORATE EACH SIDE DIFFERENTLY, IF YOU LIKE!

HANG ABOUT!

THIS BEAUTIFUL WALL HANGING IS GREAT FUN TO MAKE!

1 Paint the cardboard tubes brown so they look like sticks. Leave them to dry.

2 Work out the size of your squares by measuring the length of the cardboard tubes and dividing this measurement by three. Don't worry if it doesn't go exactly, you can round the number down so the squares are slightly smaller.

3 Cut 12 squares from different coloured pieces of paper.

4 Brush a thick layer of paint onto each square and use the end of the paintbrush to draw a pattern into the paint. You'll need to work quite quickly before the paint dries.

5 Stick the squares onto a larger sheet of paper, alternating the colours. Cut four thin pieces of coloured paper and stick them to the back of the picture, one in each corner.

6 Loop the strips of paper around the cardboard tubes and tape them to the back of the picture.

7 Thread the string or cord through the top tube and tie it in a knot. You can use this to hang up your picture!

DRAW FLOWERS, LEAVES AND INSECTS - OR ANYTHING ELSE YOU CAN FIND IN THE GARDEN!

YOU COULD EVEN USE A DIFFERENT COLOUR FOR EACH SQUARE!

I'VE USED GOLD PAINT BUT YOU CAN USE WHATEVER COLOUR YOU LIKE!

9

Petal prints!

PUT YOUR FOOT IN IT AND MAKE A GIANT FLOWER!

1 Put some paint onto a paper plate. Start with the colour you're going to use for the petals first.

2 Press the shoe into the paint then press it firmly down onto the paper. Repeat this several times until you have a circle of petals.

You will need:

Old shoes, large sheet of paper or several smaller ones taped together, cloth, paper plates, paints, paintbrush.

3 Wash the red paint off the shoe, or use another one for the stem and leaves. Use green paint this time.

4 Now use the tip of the shoe or your fingers to print the centre of the flower in brown or yellow.

5 When it's dry, hang your giant flower on the wall or the back of a door!

Bowled Over!

YOU WILL NEED:

Small bowl, Vaseline, newspaper, PVA glue, thin card, safety scissors, masking tape, paints, paintbrush.

THESE FAB BOWLS LOOK SO REAL, YOUR FRIENDS WILL BE AMAZED WHEN THEY FIND OUT THEY'RE NOT!

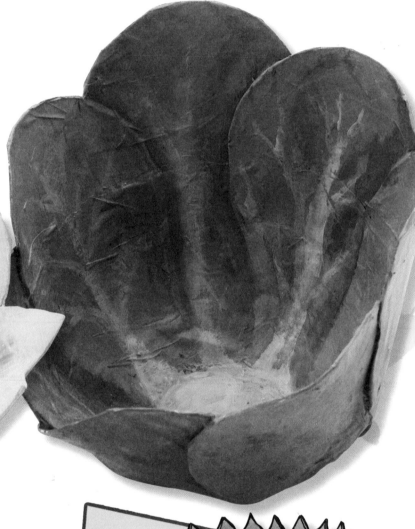

1 Before you begin, cover the outside of a bowl with a thin layer of Vaseline. Cover the bowl with three layers of papier maché and leave it to dry, then remove the bowl.

2 For the sunflower bowl, measure around the top of the papier maché and cut a piece of thin card the same length. Cut a zig-zag edge along one side and tape it place.

3

For the cabbage, cut leaf-shaped pieces from thin card and tape them around the bowl, overlapping them as shown.

4

Cover the bowls with another two layers of papier maché and leave them to dry.

5

Paint the sunflower bright yellow and add a darker brown or orange centre once the yellow paint has dried. Paint the cabbage dark green all over, adding shadow with darker paint and lighter details on the leaves.

THESE PRETTY BOWLS ARE PERFECT FOR DISPLAYING POT POURRI OR STORING SWEETS!

SUNNY DAY!

BRING SOME SUNSHINE INDOORS WITH THIS COLOURFUL GARDEN MOBILE!

YOU WILL NEED:

Thin card, glue, safety scissors, felt-tip pens, glitter glue, paints, paintbrush, string.

1 Trace or photocopy the pictures on the opposite page onto plain paper and stick them onto thin card.

2 Colour them in with felt-tip pens, adding glitter glue if you like.

3 Carefully make a hole in each piece and thread lengths of string through.

4 Lay out the pieces before tying them together, starting with the sun at the top.

5 Hang your mobile in a window or doorway and watch it twirl in the breeze!

THIS SMILEY SUN WILL BRIGHTEN UP YOUR ROOM ON A RAINY DAY!

14

TIDY TEDDIES!

MAKE TIDYING UP FUN BY STORING YOUR TOYS
IN THIS FAB HANGING BASKET!

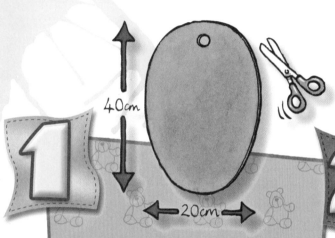

1 Cut an oval shape from cardboard box card approximately 40cm long and 20cm wide. Cut a hole for hanging at the top.

40cm

20cm

2 Cut two pieces of thin card measuring 25cm x 20cm and another oval 20cm x 10cm. Tape them together to make the basket, then tape them to the back piece, bending the edges around to make a rounded shape.

back

3 To make the raised flower motif, dip pieces of kitchen roll in diluted PVA glue and squeeze them out. Mould six petal shapes and a small ball for the centre of the flower and stick them in place.

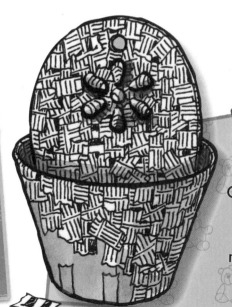

4 Cover the whole thing in two layers of papier maché and leave it to dry.

5

Paint it with a pattern of small squares in yellow and light brown, so it looks like a real basket.

Poster Paint

MAKE YOUR MARK!

KEEP YOUR PLACE WITH THESE GREAT GARDEN BOOKMARKS!

YOU WILL NEED:

Thin card, safety scissors, glue, felt-tip pens, glitter glue.

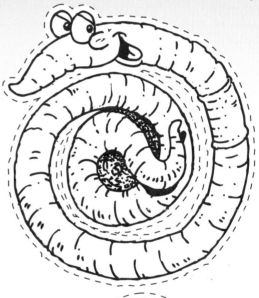

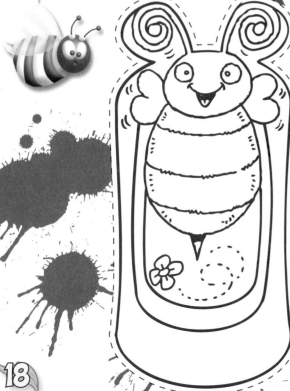

THESE ARE PERFECT FOR BOOKWORMS!

1 Trace or photocopy the bookmarks onto plain paper and stick them to a piece of thin card.

2 Colour them in using felt-tip pens. Add some glitter glue for extra sparkle, if you like.

3 Carefully cut the bookmarks out. Ask an adult to help you cut along the solid lines.

4 Now simply slot your bookmark over the top of the page in your book!

PEN PLANTER

PLANT YOUR PENS IN THIS MINIATURE GARDEN TO KEEP YOUR DESK NEAT AND TIDY!

YOU WILL NEED:

Cardboard, safety scissors, old biro, PVA glue, newspaper, masking tape, toilet roll tube, paints, paintbrush, old piece of sponge.

1 Cut a piece of card the size you want your desk tidy to be. Make two flower beds from a rectangle of card with four sides, as shown. Push an old biro through the top to make holes to store pens in, then tape them in place.

2 Cut four pieces of card for the shed walls and tape them together. I measured around a sticky note pad so it could be stored inside – approx 8cm square. Cut a lid and tape it along one side to make a hinge. Tape the shed to the base.

3 Cut down a narrow cardboard tube to make the tree stump and tape it to the base.

4 To make the pond, tape a strip of card in an oval shape to the base.

5 Cover it with two layers of papier maché, leaving the roof uncovered so it opens. Build up the edge of the pond and the hedges with extra layers. Leave it to dry.

Powder Paint

6 Paint your desk tidy as shown. Dab on green paint with an old sponge to make the grass and hedges look more realistic.

LIFT THE SHED ROOF AND STORE STICKY NOTES INSIDE!

Three-in-a-row!

YOU WILL NEED:

10 small, flat pebbles, paints, paintbrush, black marker pen, varnish, 4 straight sticks.

1
Choose two designs and paint five of each onto the pebbles. I've used flowers and leaves but you could paint anything you like. Leave them to dry, then add an outline in black marker pen.

3
Find four long, straight sticks and lay them out in a grid. Now you're ready to play!

2
When the paint is dry, brush a layer of diluted PVA glue and water over the top. When it's dry, it will act as a varnish and protect the pictures on the pebbles.

4
This is a game for two players. Take it in turns to put your pebbles in the grid. Whoever gets three in a row first is the winner!

HOW ABOUT USING DIFFERENT KINDS OF DRIED LEAVES AND PRESSED FLOWERS INSTEAD OF PEBBLES?

Nature Creatures!

CREATE THESE CRAZY CREATURES
USING THINGS YOU FIND IN THE GARDEN
OR ON A WALK IN THE PARK

YOU WILL NEED: Acorns, twigs, conkers and their shells, glue, pen, small pom-poms, googly eyes, thin black marker pen.

Silly Spider!

Push small twigs into a conker shell to make the legs. Glue on googly eyes and an acorn cup for a nose.

Conker Bug!

Glue a conker to an empty conker shell to make a head and body. Add two acorn shells at the front for feet and two more on top to make antenna. Stick on a pom-pom and googly eyes and draw a mouth with a thin black marker pen to finish.

Acorn Men!

Find some acorns with their shells still attached. These will look like little hats! Stick on googly eyes and pom-pom noses and draw a mouth using a thin black marker pen.

LOOK OUT FOR OTHER NATURAL OBJECTS YOU CAN USE WHEN YOU NEXT GO FOR A WALK!

23

Fabulous frost picture!

1 Brush the veiny sides of the dried leaves with paint and press them down onto some white paper. Remove the leaves and leave them to dry. Repeat this as many times as you like using different coloured paint.

2 When the paint is dry, use glitter glue to go over the veins. Leave them to dry again.

3 Cut a fence from silver paper or strips of foil and stick it to the background.

4 When the leaf prints are dry, cut them out and arrange these on the background, too. Stick some over the fence.

5 Dab some glue onto your picture and add frosty highlights by sprinking on glitter. Place your picture on a sheet of newspaper first to catch any extra glitter.

6 Add swirls of glitter glue and sequins for extra sparkle!

SEE HOW MANY DIFFERENT
SHAPED LEAVES YOU CAN FIND!

YOU WILL NEED:

Dried leaves, paints, paintbrush, white paper, dark paper, glitter, glue, silver paper or foil, safety scissors, glue, newspaper, sequins.

Oil Colour

YELLOW

YOU CAN USE ALL KINDS OF SHINY THINGS TO MAKE YOUR PICTURE SPARKLE! TRY MILK BOTTLE TOPS OR SCRAPS OF SHINY WRAPPING PAPER.

Finger butterflies

THESE BEAUTIFUL BUTTERFLIES ARE EASY TO MAKE AND LOTS OF FUN!

MAKE AS MANY BUTTERFLIES AS YOU LIKE!

1 Fold a piece of thin paper in half and put blobs of paint on one half. Fold the other half over and press it down. Open out the paper and leave it to dry.

2 To make the butterfly's body, roll a small tube of paper around your finger and tape it shut.

3 Fold the dry painting in half again and draw some butterfly wings on one side. Cut them out, then unfold the wings and tape them to the tube of paper.

4 Cut two thin strips of paper and curl them around a pen. Glue these inside the body to make the antenna.

POP THEM ON YOUR FINGERS AND WATCH THEM FLY!

26